Mom -

Easter
1992

from

Evelyn

Illustrated by Katie Stevenson

SPICE
FOR
LIFE

by Walt Schmidt

The C.R. Gibson Company, Norwalk, Connecticut 06856

The man who sets his goal on the highest mountain top may be climbing mountains the rest of his life. But the view from the top will always be worth the climb.

How the image of labor has changed over the years. Sweating Abe Lincoln, his sleeves rolled up, an axe slung over one shoulder ...compared with a modern pin-striped person hunched over a computing machine.

What a man could be today if there had been personal computers from the day of his birth: A man with sore fingers from daily punching on a machine.

Destiny is equipped with a handle...Someone has to crank it!

You are the pilot of your own jet plane with complicated buttons and switches on the dashboard. The most important button you must keep your finger on at all times is marked...Now!

Our town's slow, easy-going handyman is concerned about the news of a proposed four-day work week. He hopes it won't be compulsory.

The Lord expects a fair amount of physical labor. That silver shovel he handed Adam when Adam left the Garden so abruptly was for digging his path in Life...not for hanging over the fireplace.

People with sacks filled with million-dollar ideas rebel at the thought of squandering a nickel's worth of application.

A coward spends too much time thinking of what he is directly faced with. A hero is too busy doing what is necessary...to have time to think.

Doing something just to be doing something...is what America does best.

Having your life's aspirations fulfilled sometimes makes you doubt your sanity back in those early days when they were conceived.

Bless our early Mistake Makers for making the road easier for future successful efforts.

He who has not made a single mistake in his entire lifetime has not been very busy.

Speaking of total frustration...we know a young author whose novel was not only rejected but the Power Company turned off his typewriter's electricity, too!

Perhaps Rome could have
been built in a day if Nero hadn't
fiddled around so much.

Cousin Jack was extremely versatile...
could do a little of everything...badly.

The longest novel ever written comes under the title of
"I COULD HAVE BEEN..."

In these times of self-probing and identity seeking, no one can
accuse the hen of not leading a meaningful life.

The New Year does not come knocking meekly at the door.
Cowbells ring out, horns blast, people shout, auto tires screech...
reminding us that this is the year we promised to do something
different. If only we could remember what it was.

An over-achiever is a squirrel who spends all summer storing
up walnuts and all winter searching for his lost nutcracker.

We know a Mod housewife who skipped house cleaning this
spring. Couldn't feel the right vibration for picking up a broom.

Idleness requires a certain effort and adroitness in choosing
when and where to take an undisturbed siesta while honest men
employ themselves at hard labor.

Our new vice-president wasn't so much interested in his hike
in salary as he was in the privilege of taking an executive medi-
tative nap after lunch each day.

Immortality could mean you will sit an eon or two on a high heavenly cloud listening to people mispronounce your name!

Corporate tycoon to executive assistant: "Hodgins, I want you to put together a little fun basket of fruit and cookies to send to our shareholders in place of the current dividend due."

"This is a diversified company," the secretary said over the phone. "No one is ever quite sure just what we're manufacturing here."

Some of the world's greatest imaginative literary efforts can be found in the everyday expense accounts turned in by travelling salesmen.

The man who waits for fear to catch up with him might as well call an ambulance, too.

Let the world be filled with Doubting Thomases…but start worrying when it begins to be filled with Doubting Yous!

Life's most popular pastime is worry. Wealthy people can play but the poor are big wheels in the sport.

You'll never find a better sparring partner than adversity.

Thought for a workaholic: You finally stayed home because you were ill and slept the whole day through, and the world kept slowly turning on its axis and has not felt the slightest jolt.

If it's too late to seize the day and do something about it, return to your nap.

A genuine loafer is a person who gets in two morning naps before his regular afternoon nap.

Here's to the striver with a pair of ever-moving feet...the person who keeps exploring to the very last mountain trail...knowing that round every bend something wonderful waits.

No one knows for sure what the coming year will bring. Nevertheless you'll notice no one is throwing away their unused cans of fly spray.

Our town seems to be in a continuous stage of getting torn down or built up. Granted, bulldozers have to make a living, but if we could padlock a few of them for a year or two, we could have some time to enjoy what we're paying taxes for.

Our junkyard has a new sign at its entrance gate:
CITY COLLECTIBLES.

A broken parcel post package containing a box of chocolates is being held at the local post office waiting to be claimed by J. B. Hawkins, address destroyed. Better hurry...the walnut-topped fudge ones have been disappearing rapidly.

While waiting in line at our local pet shop, I heard sweet Milly Brown saying, "I'd like to exchange my canary for one that doesn't get cheerful in the middle of the night."

Pity today's bird watcher. He has to be alert for birds and muggers.

Jeb Dooley occupies the squeaky sixty-year-old rocking chair on the Country Store's porch next to the soda pop container. Tourists passing by mistake him for being in deep serious thought. But our hometowners know different...Jeb is the only man they've ever known who sleeps with his eyes wide open.

Our village park benches are crowded with Senior Citizen philosophers, horseshoe players and husbands who can't get back into their homes until their wives finish their morning housecleaning.

In a small town your face is your credit card.

Sign on tree near garage sale: Price means nothing to us. Our goal was cleaning out our attic!

Recently I hailed a cab driver who pulled over to the curb and opened the door for me. As I hopped in, the driver turned his head back to address me…"Let me introduce myself," he said. "I'm Herman your host for the duration of this ride. In my cab the rider has his choice…I talk or I sing!"

I saw a sign in our antique shop: "We have some good buys in talked-out conversation pieces."

My neighbor says our local art gallery is a marketplace where you can buy the mistakes of the old masters.

We often wonder about the rapid turnover of pretty waitresses at our favorite local restaurant…Do they retire early on the generous tips they receive, or do they marry bachelors who order the twenty-five-dollar filet mignon special with baked potatoes?

A weightwatcher friend of ours advises that: To be beautiful and slim as a reed, steamed broccoli and celery stalks is your feed.

When you're on a crash diet you do some odd things you're not aware of. Heard tell of a woman at a gypsy tearoom having her fortune told. "Read my tea leaves, please."…."I can't!" the gypsy said, "You ate them!"

Fighting boredom in a small country town is riding around the village on Saturday afternoons. Sundays…riding around the village in the opposite direction.

Our local Ladies Bridge Club held a gossip bee last Friday. Aunt Martha was voted the Fastest Mouth in Crabapple County.

Listening to what people are saying is easy. Listening to what people are thinking takes a little more concentration.

We're in favor of good news these days…even if it has to be invented.

Tattlers and busybodies who speak of things they ought not to are born television news casters.

The only "News Break" we look forward to on television is a break from the news.

SAGE FOR THE AGE

Into each life some rain must fall. If you happen to be a TV weather reporter, it falls each time you make a wrong prediction.

Put an absolute truth in the oven and it never fails to come out half-baked.

Truth never hurts...unless it won't fit into what you're trying to sell.

There's nothing as confusing as an inveterate liar who slips out with the truth now and then.

An alibi is something you spend hours preparing so you can tell it to someone who isn't listening.

While watching the Weather Report on TV last night, Grandpa commented: "You'll notice a weather forecaster and a liar have much in common. Both have to keep a straight face when they're trying to tell you something."

When you hear flattery in excess, someone is trying to be invited for supper or to sell you something.

The tongue is a small movable structure attached to the floor of the mouth. In some cases, keeping it there for a few seconds can save the day.

When two people talk at the same time, the winner is confusion.

Advice should always be consumed between two thick slices of doubt.

Who shall we believe nowadays? The doomsayer or the up-beater?...They both lie a little.

The person who interlaces his sentences with "You know! You know!" doesn't really know at all.

A smart talker knows that a nodding audience does not necessarily indicate agreement with his speech but more likely an audience falling asleep!

Psychologists tell us verbal intelligence is located in the left hemisphere of the brain. Artistic intelligence in the right hemisphere. Now we know why people keep slapping their foreheads when they're confused.

"Them psychiatrist fellows," says Clem Crubb of Hester Creek, Vermont, "take several large books crammed with thirty dollar words just to explain plain ol' wrestlin' with your soul."

There comes a time when every shoe needs repair...That goes for your soul, too.

Trivia: Useless unimportant information...everything you'll never need to know. Unless you happen to be a contestant on a TV program that gives away thousands of dollars for it.

The minister of our church would like to know: "What's all this talk about personal computers? Our Creator has been using one since the beginning of time."

Optimist: A man who refuses to tell it the way it is, today.

Laugh and the world laughs with you...cry and you've probably just finished reading the morning newspaper.

For lack of a villian to accuse...history has been blamed for all the evil that has happened in life.

As you travel through life, tattoo one tiny thought on your chest— near your ego. There are a few who are almost as smart as you and a whole lot who are much smarter than you.

The nice thing about giving advice to yourself is that it can always be self-corrected as you go along.

When an outside opinion is desired...it's just to compare how inferior it is with your own.

We spend half our lives finding out what we're incapable of doing, the other half convincing ourselves that what we are incapable of doing wasn't very interesting after all.

A man whose mind has been warped by wealth is someone who won't lend you money.

Don't dwell in the past; it's been properly buried. Don't worry about the future; it can't be bought.

Man does not invent.
He merely puts together
things invented by God.

The computer, these days,
is mightier than
the pen.

FROM THE PEPPER POT

What we need is a Surgeon General who will declare
inflation injurious to your health.

Aunt Opal declares that every time she reads a newspaper about the economy falling into a recession, the price of tomatoes goes up a few cents at her supermarket.

Tax Shelter: A complicated financial-plumbing system that flushes cash flow out of Government tax coffers.

Technical Analyst: A stock-market mystic who can accurately advise when to invest in a future-failing market and when to bail out of a future-rising market.

A Wall Street broker describes his wife as a preferred matrimonial partner of physical volume, capable of being a motivating asset if she would apply price control to capital spending.

A California bank advertises investment portfolio pruning. No doubt to spruce up your ivy-colored tax shelter.

Your local bank will take over all your financial investment problems...all that is left for you to do is sit back and worry.

Togetherness: What happens between you and your bank when you sign a long-term loan.

IRS man interviewing taxpayer: "Do you swear that all these little lies are your own and not those of a professional income tax advisor?"

Economy: Something that's always going in the wrong direction to do you any good.

Keep a stiff upper lip. Reserve the bottom lip for yelling "HELP!"

Bowing to money lenders is certain to end up giving you a pain in the neck.

It was so quiet he could hear the interest on his credit card compounding.

What this country needs is a credit card that yells "OUCH!"

Sign on our Church bulletin board: We have a large hole in our church roof caused by a falling tree in the last rainstorm. There will be a special coffee meeting Wednesday at 6 P.M. to repair same. In this case, Heaven will *not* provide. Bring your credit cards.

The old time village blacksmith could look anyone in the eye and say he owed no man a cent. Rather difficult nowadays with credit cards and offers of flying now and paying later.

It's not easy to become a Man of Letters these days. What with the price of postage...who can afford to mail a letter?

What banks used to call a luxury retirement plan, barely shapes up today as a survival kit.

Playing the stock market, if nothing else, is a creative way to lose money.

Money can build character...but not nearly as quickly as being without it.

The dollar is shrinking. If money is still going to talk, it may soon need the help of a bull horn.

There is no magical quicker-than-the-eye change as swift as your paycheck dissolving into current paid-up bills.

Sign in Clothing Store window:

BANKRUPT SALE
WHERE WERE YOU WHEN WE WERE TRYING
TO MAKE A PROFIT?

Grandpa Henley remembers the best way to save money in the old days was the slushy, rutty, hubcap-deep muddy road that prevented a family from going to town and spending it.

Hospitals are filled with modern health-repairing machines aching to be used by healthy patients.

Mother Nature heals: And does so without the help of Medicare, X-Ray machines, expensive medical education and golf clubs.

The inflated medical fees these days have developed a nation miraculously void of old-time symptoms and ailments.

After reading the family doctor book, Uncle George suffered from four ailments he never knew existed.

The new painless dentist's drill has been in operation now for some years. But the same oldfashioned screaming is still being heard when the patient receives the bill.

Our dentist just sold his television set. Found it impossible to relax with all those closeups of opera singers and politicians exposing their molars and bicuspids.

Good health doesn't come cheap. It cost me five dollars for parking fees while waiting for my doctor to return late from a golf match...to determine that healthwise I was fit as a fiddle.

Psychiatrist to male patient resting on office couch: "Now just put your head back and relax...I want you to tell me everything that comes to your mind." "Well, for the first thing," the patient said, "I see you have a dirty ceiling...needs painting...I happen to be a professional painter...Let's see now...Including the four walls that will set you back about five hundred and twenty dollars."

"He's a good doctor...but his fees are not the slightest frostbitten!"

Physician heal thyself...
and don't forget to jack up
the fee three times
its worth.

Looking through an ancient mail order catalogue, we were impressed with the miracle-medicines of earlier days. For the sum of sixty cents you could purchase a bottle of Dr. Hammond's Nerve and Brain Pills guaranteed to cure you of low spirits, headaches, specks before the eyes, poor memory, palpitation of the heart, cold feet, hot flashes and rumbling stomach...a bargain anyway you look at it. Sixty cents today would hardly take care of your parking meter while you were waiting for the pharmacist to fill your prescription—worth its weight in gold.

A psychologist suggests that trying to be an agreeable fellow may halt emotional growth. It's going to be tough breaking this news to our politicians.

Our ecological campaign to recycle wastepaper is nothing new ...The Congressional Record has been doing this for years.

Nothing is sure in this world but death and taxes and the politician's promise to lower the latter just before election time.

A politician who claims he is making a speech that will benefit both rich and poor ends up talking to himself.

How the meaning of words changes with time. In the old days it was called graft...nowadays, fiscal impropriety.

Our Senator says the greatest boon to public speaking is the address system that breaks down now and then.

Washington Senator to his speechwriter: "Instead of telling them to bite the bullet and tighten the belt...let's just tell them to stay home and stop spending money!"

GRATE ONE LEMON

Our neighbor just bought two new cars: a standard-sized one and a compact he drives when he's on a diet.

Detroit tells us that big cars are coming back. Even so, it'll take a couple of years to get the crink out of the backs of drivers of compacts.

Our local health gym announced a new class on the art of getting in and out of mini-compact cars.

As we drove into our favorite gas station this morning, we parked directly behind a sweet little old lady sitting behind the wheel of an ancient model. She was smiling as the station man approached her with a tire gauge. "Would you mind fluffing up my tires a bit?" she asked politely.

When a man hangs on to the same car for over thirty years, you have to guess that he's a close relative of Mister Goodwrench.

Customer to second-hand car dealer: "I have a sore toe...would you mind kicking that tire for me?"

Sign on second-hand auto lot:
PLEASE DON'T KICK OUR TIRES...
WHAT DID THEY EVER DO TO YOU?

Three signs at gas station:
 1st sign: Full Service
 2nd sign: Self Service
 3rd sign: Just driving through while
          checking new gas prices.

As the twig is bent...usually indicates a path where our teenage driver has just driven out of the garage...the wrong way.

Recently I overhead a driver on the Full Service side of a gas station complain to the attendant, "I'm paying 5 cents more a gallon and all you do is tighten my radiator cap and collect money for the gas!" "Just wait, M'am," the attendant smiled. "When you leave the station, notice how I wave goodbye to you."

Mechanic to Auto Owner: "You'd better sit down while I tell you what all of this is going to cost you."

Overheard at Yellowstone Park Rangers' Headquarters: Tourist camper in pajamas: "Ranger, is there anyway you can turn these crickets off?"

I'm not one to dig up new things to worry about...but I've often wondered what happens when you drive your car through one of those Lion Safari parks and get a flat tire?

What the auto industry needs desperately is a new car bumper that bumper stickers won't stick to.

If you are in no hurry and would like to see the rest of the world …just ask any stranger for directions.

All's fair in love and war and highway driving.

Our Congressman is at his Capitol Hill office early each morning, knee-deep in touring maps, trying to figure out the best scenic route for his next political junket.

Middle-age is when you need to ask a teenager for instructions at a Self-Help gas pump.

After wrecking the drive-in teller's booth a second time, our local bank asked Aunt Stella to make her deposits elsewhere.

We applaud the airline tourist who couldn't make up his mind where to go on a vacation. Finally settled on going to wherever his baggage was delivered to.

Aging is something that happens to other people.

You can't teach an old dog new tricks…not while the old tricks are working so well!

Age cannot be computed by an adding machine. How you feel and think can make a liar out of common figures.

Life begins at forty…the kind of life you've dreaded thinking about for the last forty years.

Realizing that age has finally caught up with you should be a pleasant experience. Looking up from a nearly finished book, through the frosted window we see our world newly covered with winter snow. There it is whether we like it or not…and there's nothing we can do to change it.

Your confirmed membership in the OVER THE HILL club starts when you keep asking, "Who's that?" during the Oscar Awards.

A Senator answered a voice on his phone: "You say this is my conscience speaking?…Do you mind if I put you on hold?"

Misplaced pride is the Senior Citizen who refuses to show his AARP card for a ten percent discount at the movie theatre.

Much as we'd like to…there's no one we can sue for growing old.

What adventurous fools we were in our youth. We couldn't wait to explore any path that was forbidden.

Ancient Ben Tucker, 97, says he'd be all for thinking young…if he could get his back and legs to think the same way.

Ted Jones, our next door neighbor, doesn't go for college kid stuff. "For four years they stuff their brains full of new ways of staying out of work permanently," he claims.

Today's youth wouldn't blink an eyelash if Jupiter hurled his thunderbolts continuously day and night. They're too busy playing TV Super-Spaceman games and listening to ear-shattering rock music.

Our nation's energy problem would be solved if there were only some way we could harness the energy generated by rock musicians.

Notice how the face of a musician suffers as he plays his violin? If he happens to be a bad violinist, notice how that same expression transfers to the audience's faces.

"Now hear this!" the camp director said over the public address system to small scouts packing their suitcases. "We are now packing up our things for the trip home...*Things*...I *repeat*... does *not* include *snakes* and *toads!*"

Heavenly Choir speaking: SORRY, NO ELECTRIC GUITARS!

Try not to worry about what youth will think of next. For certain you'll know it will be outrageous and shocking.

Gray hair means simply that if you are going to have wisdom in this life, you should be getting some right about now.

We know a school teacher who takes Karate lessons for security reasons...and her students are only third graders.

Music: Living echoes of our yesterdays.

Youth dances because it can't help but dance.
Others dance just to find out whether they are
still able to.

Growing old is not all that easy.
Have you ever tried ballet
dancing with the help of a cane?

We're taking a course in speed-reading so we can keep up with
our junk-mail.

For that lived-in look, nothing can compare with the old family
stepladder splotched with various colored paints, leaning against
the basement wall.

Amateur gardeners not only have green thumbs but purple knees.

Our "How To" garden book tells us to spray after each rainstorm,
but gives us no instructions on how to mop up a muddy kitchen
floor after returning from the garden.

In the warmer States, February is the time to buy and plant bare-
root roses…"Profusely blooming pink…Breathtaking beauty" the
ads assure…but good fortune will be yours if more than
half mature.

The wind-blown bamboo on our patio is the first sight my eyes behold early each morning. As I lie here generating enough courage to climb out of bed, the leaves tremble with each new breath of morning wind—forming magic images. The green foliage-face of a remarkably beautiful woman smiles at me this morning. The sudden movement of the wind makes her lips appear as though she is trying to tell me something. Could it be Mother Nature herself, calling her Jolly Green Giant to get up and mow the lawn?

Gardening is the only occupation where a man can stand motionless for a long stretch of time studying his flowers without being accused of being a loafer.

Uncle Charlie says that loving one's neighbor sometimes depends on the variety of workable garden tools he has available for lending.

There's nothing more demanding than a slow leak in the living room ceiling.

A young housewife to her plumber said: "If it's going to be expensive...*you're* the one who's going to have to explain it to my husband!"

After having had to call the plumber six times during the past week, the housewife opened her front door to greet him a seventh time on Saturday. "Good morning!" she laughed, "I have a feeling we're going steady!"

Our basement plumbing pipes are beginning to sound off with a sonata of weird noises. No doubt timed to coincide with the last installment due on our current plumbing bill.

Only those who were with Noah in the Ark remained alive. And the waters prevailed on the earth one hundred and fifty days. We can see Noah shaking his head in disbelief as he walked down the gangplank to dry earth. "Man!" he shouted, "This is the longest I've ever had to wait for the plumber."

When plumbers finally appear at the heavenly pearly gates, do they present a portal-to-portal traveling charge?

Blessed is he who never has had to argue with his landlord while holding a thumb over a gushing water faucet.

One-eighth of an inch doesn't sound like much...but it's enough to make a carpenter lose his job.

When your house shines like a new dime, it shows you don't particularly trust the guests you've invited to your dinner party.

A home should be a cooperative enterprise...each member with a recognized share in the operation. Like, a husband should have control of the TV monitor that switches a soap opera to a football game.

Storm doors are what you carefully take down and store up in the attic the day before the greatest blizzard of the century.

Aunt Jenny feels certain there's something terrible about to happen in this world...Miggs, her Cheshire cat, has lost her grin lately and is affecting a definite sneer.

An acoustical engineer friend of ours has sound-proofed his home to a point of perfection...can't even hear his wife shouting at him from the kitchen.

Bank Loan officer to prospective home buyers: "Now do you two solemnly swear if this mortgage is granted, you will give up smoking and drinking, take on part-time moonlighting jobs and squirrel up all the money you can lay hands on to pay it off?"

Our Congressman needs no dance instructor to teach him the latest Disco dance. Each morning he has to go through the same body movements getting through the hordes of protesters crowded on the front steps leading to the Capitol building.

The report is that our Congressman is giving consideration to running for the nomination for U.S. Senate...a consideration he has been considering since the day he graduated from law school.

The rattling of swords is so loud these days it's hard to make out what the diplomats are saying.

If there were no great leaders in this world, there would be no great wars.

The United Nations should pass a law that prohibits a new war before the old one is paid for.

Uninspiring labels for the elderly: Senior Citizen, Septuagenarian, Octogenarian. Let's abolish them in favor of a more respectful title like M.S.: "Majestic Survivor."

A DROP OF HONEY

Writing love letters is like banking. Each letter becomes a gilt-edged deposit drawing compound interest on a lifelong marriage.

Love is a many splintered thing.

Never to have been in love simply means a man needs a new pair of glasses.

As to our gasoline-saving problem, you won't find a more patriotic group than in our local lovers' lane.

The best way out of a difficulty is never to marry one in the first place.

Bachelor: A man who always keeps a pilot light burning on the altar of Love.

Love is two people who can't get along with each other, discovering they can't get along without each other.

Our teenage daughter can't make up her mind whether she's in love or has a case of Hong Kong flu.

Our next door neighbor, known for being a wag of sorts, pretends he knows nothing about the reply his pretty daughter's numerous boyfriends get over the phone..."Dan, Billy, Joe or Ted...Doris is not home...Doris is not home...This is a recording..."

Young girl to boyfriend: "Let's be perfectly honest...We met at a computer dating agency...Now I'm punching you out of my life!"

"Gone fishin'" has often saved a marriage from "going bankrupt."

Harmony need not be limited to singing quartets.

Love not just your own family…but the world where your own family came from.

There's nothing briefer than a present-day family conference on what to do with surplus money.

Family-Get-Together: What happens when the family TV breaks down and the set is required to go to the repair shop for three days.

His wife could tolerate his being retired and hanging around the house…until he installed a "Suggestion" box in the kitchen.

Housewife shopper to supermarket manager: "Do you have any spray that'll keep my husband out of the house for a couple of hours?"

Our new trend of conglomerating our business industries is old hat to a housewife experienced in dealing in diversified labors such as wife, mother, bookkeeper, laundress, chauffeur, and shopper.

Mother's Day: The day when all her children pack up and take a train to the State University.

The wife of a friend of mine is checking out her husband's enthusiasm for aerobic exercise-dancing with female instructors. "And after thirty years of trying to push him out on a dance floor at parties!" she protests.

Genealogy: An attempt to account for the number of old-time horse thieves hanging from your family tree.

A bookkeeper made up his own announcement card for his family's recent blessed event:

Gratefully announcing a new
fixed monthly expense to the
Smith family's budget:

Mary Ann   2/12/85   8lbs.6oz.

We are thankful to our college-age daughter for advising her mother and me on how to survive this ecological modern world. Gives you a chill though, wondering how my wife and I managed to muddle through this far.

If you were handed a dictionary and asked to choose just two words from it that would protect and comfort you for the rest of your life...what better choice than *courage* and *love*?

On our Saturday morning walk through the village, we noticed our daughter has picked up that trick teenage girls have taught themselves: walking through town with her nose up in the air... and at the same time admiring her reflection in a store display window... and counting the number of boys watching her from across the street.

Our teen daughter and the girl next door are not speaking to each other. Seems they compared daydreams. A certain boyfriend was in both of them.

The way to your teenage daughter's heart is a walk through a shopping mall clutching a brand-new, unused credit card.

Gilding the modern lily can be time consuming. Our teenage daughter spent most of the afternoon deciding whether to wear "wispy" or "full-fluffy" eyelashes to the Spring Prom.

How come a teenage baseball player can remember every play he's made that season but hesitates when it comes to remembering whether or not he took out the morning trash can?

With newspapers and TV outpouring millions of exciting words about baseball each season, you'd think Webster's dictionary could have used a little more enthusiasm than describing it as a game played with a hard rawhide-covered ball and wooden bat by two opposing teams of nine players.

Inheritance is a jackpot you win when you're lucky enough to have been related to the right person.

There is only one word in a three-year-old's dictionary... ACTION.

Your greatest shining hour is when someone is showing photos of their grandchildren. True gentleman that you are, you allow a generous allotment of time for listening to description, praise and adoration before you counter-attack with a fat photo wallet of your own superior grandchild.

The hand on the wall keeps writing...but nowadays it puts it neatly in an envelope and mails it to you each day..."You *may* already have won the $100,000 Sweepstakes or $10,000 a week for the rest of your life!"

"I'm not saying that nature's animals are racist...but our dog considers the morning unfinished until he chases the neighbor's cat up a tree.

There is nothing wrong with a cat except her decision to take a nap on the exact spot of the sofa you are about to sit down on.

"Dinner is ready!" a feminine voice calls from the kitchen. Family bodies start moving towards the dining room. No one knows more certain than Mom the exact split second when a kitchen full of boiling pots and sizzling skillets have reached their peak. It's an art and the family gratefully acknowledges it. But what the whole family doesn't realize is that Mom would gladly relinquish her culinary magic now and then to enjoy the fun of being waited on.

I never realized how binding family relationships could be until we attended our annual family picnic this year at Palmer's Grove. Our eight-year-old nephew, Billy, was concerned over returning coffee refills to the proper owners. Suddenly he brightened and said, "It doesn't matter anyway; we all have the same germs!"

The finest moment of your finest hour is when your very young son, playing an angel in a Christmas play, stops whatever he is reciting and grins out at you as he points his finger in your direction and shouts "Daddy!"

Love is not a statement of the mind.
It is barely audible,
Mixed with soft music that ends in a whisper,
No more, or less...
Leaving a permanent smile
inside your heart.

My wife's smile has a 40,000 mile warranty and, luckily for me, she delights in using up every mile of it.